My Diary of an Oak Tree

Mark McArthur-Christie

Contents

Oxford

Oxford University Press, Great Clarendon Street, Oxford, OX2 6DP

Oxford New York
Athens Auckland Bangkok Bogota Buenos Aires
Calcutta Cape Town Chennai Dar es Salaam Delhi
Florence Hong Kong Istanbul Karachi Kuala Lumpur
Madrid Melbourne Mexico City Mumbai Nairobi Paris
São Paulo Singapore Taipei Tokyo Toronto Warsaw

and associated companies in
Berlin Ibadan

Oxford is a trade mark of Oxford University Press

Text © Mark McArthur-Christie 1999
Published by Oxford University Press 1999
A CIP record for this book is available from the British Library

ISBN 0 19 915769 3
Available in packs
Pack B Pack of Six   (one of each book)   ISBN 0 19 915771 5
Pack B Class Pack   (six of each book)   ISBN 0 19 915772 3

Acknowledgements

The publisher would like to thank the following for permission
to reproduce photographs: Biofotos/Heather Angel: p 5 (bottom
right); Bruce Coleman Collection/Kim Taylor: pp 5 (bottom left),
9; Corbis UK Ltd/ Joe McDonald: p 11 (middle); Corbis UK
Ltd/Nigel J Dennis: p 11 (top); Corbis UK Ltd/George Lepp: p 5
(top); Oxford Scientific Films/Michael Leach: p 11 (bottom);
Planet Earth Pictures/Hedley Charles: p 7; Telegraph Colour
Library/Planet Earth/John Lythgoe: pp 3, 4, 6, 8, 10.

Front cover photograph by Telegraph Colour Library/Planet
Earth/John Lythgoe.
Back cover photograph by Corbis UK Ltd/Papilio/Neil Miller.
Illustrations by Julie Tolliday.

With special thanks to Ian Harvey, Forestry Authority.

Printed in Hong Kong

Introduction

The oak tree near my house changed through the year. This is my diary about it.

Spring

In spring, leaves and flowers grew on my oak tree. Lots of animals lived in it.

gall wasp

robin

caterpillar

Summer

In summer, the leaves turned dark green. Birds nested in the branches and had chicks.

robin feeding
its chicks ■

Tree roots get their
food from the soil.

ants' nest ●

root hairs

Autumn

In autumn, the leaves turned red and brown. Acorns fell off the tree.

beefsteak fungus 🔴

How an acorn grows ⬛

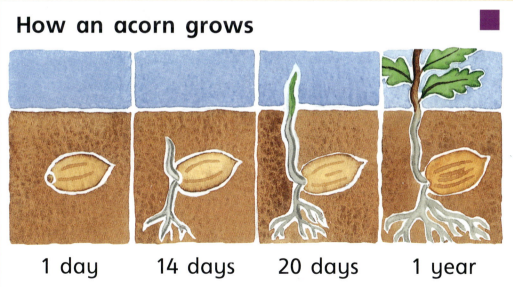

| 1 day | 14 days | 20 days | 1 year |

Acorns are the seeds of oak trees.

Winter

In winter, the leaves fell off.
It was hard for the animals to
find food.

badger sett

squirrel drey

woodmouse

Index